HAMLET

Shakespeare The Animated Tales is a multinational venture conceived by S4C, Channel 4 Wales. Produced in Russia, Wales and England, the series has been financed by S4C, the BBC and HIT Communications (UK), Christmas Films and Soyuzmultfilm (Russia), Home Box Office (USA) and Fujisankei (Japan).

Academic Panel
Professor Stanley Wells
Dr Rex Gibson

Academic Co-ordinator
Roy Kendall

Educational Adviser
Michael Marland

Publishing Editor and Co-ordinator
Jane Fior

Book Design
Fiona Macmillan

Animation Director for *Hamlet*
Natalia Orlova of Soyuzmultfilm Studios, Moscow

Series Producer and Director
Dave Edwards of The Dave Edwards Studio Ltd, Cardiff

Executive Producers
Christopher Grace
Elizabeth Babakhina

First published in 1992
by William Heinemann Ltd
an imprint of Egmont Children's Books Ltd
Michelin House, 81 Fulham Road, London SW3 6RB
10 9 8 7 6 5 4
Text and illustrations copyright © Shakespeare Animated Films Ltd
Christmas Joint Venture and Soyuzmultfilm 1992
ISBN 0 434 96231 7
Printed in Hong Kong

The publishers would like to thank Paul Cox for
the use of his illustration of The Globe and
the series logo illustration, Carole Kempe for
her calligraphy, Patrick Spottiswoode for his
introduction and Elizabeth Laird, Ness Wood,
Rosa Fior and Jillian Boothroyd for their help
in the production of the books.

Shakespeare
THE ANIMATED TALES

HAMLET

ABRIDGED BY
LEON GARFIELD

ILLUSTRATED BY
NATALIA ORLOVA, PETER KOTOV
AND NATASHA DEMIDOVA

HEINEMANN YOUNG BOOKS

THE THEATRE IN SHAKESPEARE'S DAY

IN 1989 AN ARCHAEOLOGICAL discovery was made on the south bank of the Thames that sent shivers of delight through the theatre world. A fragment of Shakespeare's own theatre, the Globe, where many of his plays were first performed, had been found.

This discovery has fuelled further interest in how Shakespeare himself conceived and staged his plays. We know a good deal already, and archaeology as well as documentary research will no doubt reveal more, but although we can only speculate on some of the details, we have a good idea of what the Elizabethan theatre-goer saw, heard and smelt when he went to see a play by William Shakespeare at the Globe.

It was an entirely different experience from anything we know today. Modern theatres have roofs to keep out the weather. If it rained on the Globe, forty per cent of the play-goers got wet. Audiences today sit on cushioned seats, and usually (especially if the play is by Shakespeare) watch and listen in respectful silence. In the Globe, the floor of the theatre was packed with a riotous crowd of garlic-reeking apprentices, house servants and artisans, who had each paid a penny to stand for the entire duration of the play, to buy nuts and apples from the food-sellers, to refresh themselves with bottled ale, relieve themselves, perhaps, into buckets by the back wall, to talk, cheer, catcall, clap and hiss if the play did not please them.

In the galleries, that rose in curved tiers around the inside of the building, sat those who could afford to pay two pennies for a seat, and the benefits of a roof over their heads. Here, the middle ranking citizens, the merchants, the sea captains, the clerks from the Inns of Court, would sit crammed into their small eighteen inch space and look down upon the 'groundlings' below. In the 'Lords room', the rich and the great, noblemen and women, courtiers and foreign ambassadors had to pay sixpence each for the relative comfort and luxury of their exclusive position directly above the stage, where they smoked tobacco, and overlooked the rest.

We are used to a stage behind an arch, with wings on either side, from which the actors come on and into which they disappear. In the Globe, the stage was a platform thrusting out into the middle of the floor, and the audience, standing in the central yard, surrounded it on three sides. There were no wings. Three doors at the back of the stage were used for all exits and entrances. These were sometimes covered by a curtain, which could be used as a prop as when Polonious, eavesdropping on Hamlet and the Queen, hides himself behind the curtain, and is run through by Hamlet's sword.

Today we sit in a darkened theatre or cinema, and look at a brilliantly lit stage or screen, or we sit at home in a small, private world of our own, watching a luminous television screen. The close-packed, rowdy crowd at the Globe, where the play started at two o'clock in the afternoon, had no artificial light to enhance their illusion. It was the words that moved them. They came to listen, rather than to see.

No dimming lights announced the start of the play. A blast from a trumpet and three sharp knocks warned the audience that the action was about to begin. In the broad daylight, the actor could see the audience as clearly as the audience could see him. He spoke directly to the crowd, and held them with his eyes, following their reactions. He could play up to the raucous laughter that greeted the comical, bawdy scenes, and gauge the emotional response to the higher flights of poetry. Sometimes he even improvised speeches of his own. He was surrounded by, enfolded by his audience.

The stage itself would seem uncompromisingly bare to our eyes. There was no scenery. No painted backdrops suggested a forest, or a castle, or the sumptuous interior of a palace. Shakespeare painted the scenery with his words, and the imagination of the audience did the rest.

Props were brought onto the stage only when they were essential for the action. A bed would be carried on when a character needed to lie on it. A throne would be let down from above when a king needed to sit on it. Torches and lanterns would suggest that it was dark, but the main burden of persuading an audience, at three o'clock in the afternoon, that it was in fact the middle of the night, fell upon the language.

In our day, costume designers create a concept as part of the production of a play into which each costume fits. Shakespeare's actors were responsible for their own costumes. They would use what was to hand in the 'tiring house' (dressing room), or supplement it out of their own pockets. Classical, medieval and Tudor clothes could easily appear side by side in the same play.

No women actors appeared on a public stage until many years after Shakespeare's death, for at that time it would have been considered shameless. The parts of young girls were played by boys. The parts of older women were played by older men.

In 1613 the Globe theatre was set on fire by a spark from a cannon during a performance of Henry VIII, and it burnt to the ground. The actors, including Shakespeare himself, dug into their own pockets and paid for it to be rebuilt. The new theatre lasted until 1642, when it closed again. Now, in the 1990s, the Globe is set to rise again as a committed band of actors, scholars and enthusiasts are raising the money to rebuild Shakespeare's theatre in its original form a few yards from its previous site.

From the time when the first Globe theatre was built until today, Shakespeare's plays have been performed in a vast variety of languages, styles, costumes and techniques, on stage, on film, on television and in animated film. Shakespeare himself, working within the round wooden walls of his theatre, would have been astonished by it all.

PATRICK SPOTTISWOODE
Director of Education,
Globe Theatre Museum

WILLIAM SHAKESPEARE

NEXT TO GOD, A wise man once said, Shakespeare created most. In the thirty-seven plays that are his chief legacy to the world — and surely no-one ever left a richer! — human nature is displayed in all its astonishing variety.

He has enriched the stage with matchless comedies, tragedies, histories, and, towards the end of his life, with plays that defy all description, strange plays that haunt the imagination like visions.

His range is enormous: kings and queens, priests, princes and merchants, soldiers, clowns and drunkards, murderers, pimps, whores, fairies, monsters and pale, avenging ghosts 'strut and fret their hour upon the stage'. Murders and suicides abound; swords flash, blood flows, poison drips, and lovers sigh; yet there is always time for old men to talk of growing apples and for gardeners to discuss the weather.

In the four hundred years since they were written, they have become known and loved in every land; they are no longer the property of one country and one people, they are the priceless possession of the world.

His life, from what we know of it, was not astonishing. The stories that have attached themselves to him are remarkable only for their ordinariness: poaching deer, sleeping off a drinking bout under a wayside tree. There are no duels, no loud, passionate loves, no excesses of any kind. He was not one of your unruly geniuses whose habits are more interesting than their works. From all accounts, he was of a gentle, honourable disposition, a good businessman, and a careful father.

He was born on April 23rd 1564, to John and Mary Shakespeare of Henley Street, Stratford-upon-Avon. He was their third child and first son. When he was four or five he began his education at the local petty school. He left the local grammar school when he was about fourteen, in all probability to help in his father's glove-making shop. When he was eighteen, he married Anne Hathaway, who lived in a nearby village. By the time he was twenty-one, he was the father of three children, two daughters and a son.

Then, it seems, a restless mood came upon him. Maybe he travelled, maybe he was, as some say, a schoolmaster in the country; but at some time during the next seven years, he went to London and found employment in the theatre. When he was twenty-eight, he was already well enough known as an actor and playwright to excite the spiteful envy of a rival, who referred to him as 'an upstart crow'.

He mostly lived and worked in London until his mid-forties, when he returned to his family and home in Stratford, where he remained in prosperous circumstances until his death on April 23rd 1616, his fifty-second birthday.

He left behind him a widow, two daughters (his son died in childhood), and the richest imaginary world ever created by the human mind.

LEON GARFIELD

HAMLET

More books have been written about Hamlet than about any other story ever told: for Hamlet is Everyman, who questions the very reason for his own existence: 'To be, or not to be...' Set in Denmark, long ago, it is a tale of revenge; of a prince who is called upon, by the ghost of his dead father, to avenge his father's murder by the hand of his uncle, who is now the king.

Shakespeare took the story from the work of an old Danish historian, and, like all his borrowings, the debt was repaid a thousandfold. He takes pebbles, as was said of the composer Handel, and gives back diamonds.

Shakespeare wrote it, probably, when he was about thirty-seven or thirty-eight; but the date, like everything else in this play, is uncertain. Doubt and mystery stalk its pages, like the ghost that stalks the battlements. Is the ghost an 'honest ghost', or is it a 'goblin damned'? Does the queen know of her husband's crime, or is she, like others, an innocent victim? And at the very heart of things is Prince Hamlet himself—surely the most brilliant and complex character ever put upon the stage! Although he tells us what is in his mind, we never truly know what is in his heart. 'You would pluck out the heart of my mystery,' he accuses a seeming friend; and then denies the possibility of any such thing: 'You can fret me, you cannot play upon me.'

For many, many years now, scholars, poets and psychologists have fretted at Hamlet; but the brooding, black-clad prince somehow eludes them all. Why does he delay in his revenge? He does not seem to know himself. Time and again he asks himself that question, and the only answer he can provide is that he thinks too much: 'the native hue of resolution is sicklied o'er with the pale cast of thought.'

A strange hero; yet one who lives in the mind like no other: a pale young man standing on the battlements of an ancient castle, under a night sky, crying out bitterly, as if to an unjust God, 'the time is out of joint: O cursed spite that ever I was born to set it right.'

THE CHARACTERS IN THE PLAY

in order of appearance

MARCELLUS BARNADO	*members of the King's guard*
GHOST	*of the late King, Hamlet's father*
HORATIO	*friend and confidant of Hamlet*
HAMLET	*Prince of Denmark*
CLAUDIUS	*King of Denmark, Hamlet's uncle*
LAERTES	*Polonius' son*
POLONIUS	*a councillor of state*
GERTRUDE	*the Queen, Hamlet's mother, now wife of Claudius*
OPHELIA	*Polonius' daughter*
(THE PLAYER KING) (THE PLAYER QUEEN) (MURDERER)	*players*
SOLDIER	
GRAVEDIGGER	
COURTIER	
JUDGE	
SERVANT	

(Names in brackets indicate non-speaking parts)

The curtain rises on the battlements of a dark and forbidding castle. It is night. Three figures are huddled together. They are Marcellus and Barnardo, sentinels, and Horatio, a visitor to the castle. They are staring fearfully about them.

MARCELLUS   Look where it comes again!

Out of the swirling nothingness comes a ghostly figure, all in armour. Slowly it stalks by; and its face, seen beneath its helmet, is filled with gloom.

BARNARDO   In the same figure like the king that's dead!

MARCELLUS   Is it not like the king, Horatio?

HORATIO   As thou art to thyself. (*The apparition vanishes.*) Let us impart what we have seen unto young Hamlet.

They all stare after the vanished phantom.

MARCELLUS   Something is rotten in the state of Denmark.

In the royal council chamber, the king and queen sit fondly side by side. Behind them stands Polonius, the doting old Lord Chamberlain. The brightly coloured court looks smiling on. But one figure sits apart, and all in black. It is Prince Hamlet. He stares at his mother, the queen, then turns away.

HAMLET (*to himself*) That it should come to this! A little month, or ere those shoes were old with which she followed my poor father's body—O God, a beast that wants discourse of reason would have mourned longer!—married to my uncle, my father's brother, but no more like my father than I to Hercules!

As he murmurs to himself, a young man of the court comes and kneels before the king.

KING What wouldst thou beg, Laertes?

LAERTES My dread lord, your leave and favour to return to France.

KING Have you your father's leave? What says Polonius?

POLONIUS He hath, my lord, wrung from me my slow leave.

KING Take thy fair hour, Laertes. (*Laertes bows and withdraws.*) But now my cousin Hamlet, and my son—

HAMLET (*aside*) A little more than kin, and less than kind.

KING —how is it that the clouds still hang upon you?

QUEEN   Good Hamlet, cast thy nighted colour off. Do not for ever seek for thy noble father in the dust. Thou know'st 'tis common: all that lives must die.

HAMLET   Ay, madam, it is common.

QUEEN   If it be, why seems it so particular with thee?

HAMLET   Seems, madam? Nay, it is. I know not 'seems'.

KING   'Tis sweet and commendable in your nature, Hamlet, to give these mourning duties to your father, but you must know your father lost a father, that father lost, lost his.—We pray you, throw to earth this unprevailing woe . . .

Hamlet stares at him. The king sighs, and, with his queen, leaves the chamber, followed by the court.

HAMLET   Frailty, thy name is woman!

Enter Horatio, Barnardo and Marcellus. Hamlet smiles.

HAMLET   Horatio, or I do forget myself! But what is your affair in Elsinore?

HORATIO   My lord, I came to see your father's funeral.

HAMLET   I prithee, do not mock me, fellow-student. I think it was to see my mother's wedding.

HORATIO   Indeed, my lord, it followed hard upon.

HAMLET   Thrift, thrift, Horatio. The funeral baked meats did coldly
          furnish forth the marriage tables! (*He sighs and gazes into the
          distance.*) My father—methinks I see my father—

HORATIO   Where, my lord?

HAMLET   In my mind's eye, Horatio.

HORATIO   My lord, I think I saw him yesternight.

HAMLET   Saw? Who? For God's love let me hear!

HORATIO   Two nights together had these gentlemen on their watch been
          thus encountered. A figure like your father, armed at point
          exactly, appears before them, and with solemn march goes
          slow and stately by them. Thrice he walked. I knew your
          father, these hands are not more like.

HAMLET   But where was this?

MARCELLUS   My lord, upon the platform where we watched.

HAMLET   Stayed it long?

HORATIO   While one with moderate haste might tell a hundred.

MARCELLUS
AND BARNARDO   (*shaking their heads*) Longer, longer!

HORATIO	Not when I saw it.
HAMLET	I will watch tonight, perchance 'twill walk again. Fare you well. (*Horatio and his companions withdraw*.) My father's spirit, in arms! All is not well!

A room in the castle. Laertes, prepared for France, is bidding farewell to Ophelia, his sister.

LAERTES	My necessaries are embarked, farewell. And sister, do not sleep but let me hear from you.
OPHELIA	Do you doubt that?
LAERTES	For Hamlet, and the trifling of his favour, hold it a fashion, and a toy in the blood, no more.
OPHELIA	No more but so?
LAERTES	Fear it, Ophelia, fear it, my dear sister, and keep you in the rear of his affection . . . But here my father comes!

Enter Polonius, full of bustle and importance.

POLONIUS	Yet here, Laertes? Aboard, aboard for shame! The wind sits in the shoulder of your sail, and you are stayed for! There, my blessing with thee!
LAERTES	Farewell, Ophelia, and remember well what I have said to you.
OPHELIA	'Tis in my memory locked.

LAERTES	Farewell. (*He embraces her, and departs.*)
POLONIUS	What is't, Ophelia, he hath said to you?
OPHELIA	So please you, something touching the Lord Hamlet.
POLONIUS	What is't between you? Give me up the truth.
OPHELIA	He hath, my lord, of late made many tenders of his affections to me.
POLONIUS	Affection? Pooh, you speak like a green girl!
OPHELIA	My lord, he hath importuned me with love in honourable fashion.
POLONIUS	Go to, go to! From this time be somewhat scanter of your maiden presence. I would not, in plain terms, from this time forth, have you so slander any moment leisure as to give words or talk with the Lord Hamlet. Look to it, I charge you!
OPHELIA	I shall obey you.

Night on the battlements. Hamlet, Horatio and Marcellus stand together.

HAMLET	What hour now?
HORATIO	I think it lacks of twelve.
MARCELLUS	No, it is struck.

HORATIO	Indeed, I heard it not. It then draws near the season wherein the spirit held his wont to walk. (*They stare into the dark.*) Look, my lord, it comes!

The ghost appears, and stalks towards Hamlet.

HAMLET	Angels and ministers of grace defend us! (*The ghost beckons.*) I will follow it!
HORATIO	Do not, my lord!
HAMLET	Why, what should be the fear? I do not set my life at a pin's fee, and for my soul, what can it do to that, being a thing immortal as itself. I'll follow it!
MARCELLUS	You shall not, my lord!
HORATIO	Be ruled: you shall not go!

They try to restrain Hamlet. He frees himself and draws his sword.

HAMLET	By heaven, I'll make a ghost of him that lets me! I say away!

The ghost, ever beckoning to Hamlet, mounts steps towards a high, lonely platform. Hamlet follows.

HAMLET	Go on, I'll follow thee!

The platform is reached. Hamlet's companions have been left behind. Hamlet is alone with the ghost.

GHOST   I am thy father's spirit, doomed for a certain time to walk the night, and for the day confined to fast in fires, till the foul crimes done in my days of nature are burnt and purged away. (*Hamlet buries his face in his hands in horror.*) List, list, O list! If thou didst ever thy dear father love—

HAMLET   O God!

GHOST   Revenge his foul and most unnatural murder!

HAMLET   Murder!

GHOST   Murder most foul, as in the best it is. Now, Hamlet, hear. 'Tis given out that, sleeping in my orchard, a serpent stung me. But know thou, noble youth, the serpent that did sting thy father's life now wears his crown.

HAMLET   O my prophetic soul! My uncle!

GHOST   Ay, that incestuous, that adulterous beast, with witchcraft of his wit, with traitorous gifts, won to his shameful lust, the will of my most seeming virtuous queen. O Hamlet, what a falling-off was there! Let not the royal bed of Denmark be a couch for luxury and damned incest! But howsoever thou pursuest this act, taint not thy mind nor let thy soul contrive against thy mother aught. Leave her to Heaven . . . Fare thee well . . . Adieu, adieu, adieu. Remember me.

Little by little, the ghost fades into nothingness. Hamlet is left alone, weeping with grief, pity and rage.

HAMLET   Remember thee? Ay, thou poor ghost, whiles memory holds a seat in this distracted globe! (*He rushes to the edge of the platform and glares down towards the dark bulk of the castle, from which lights and faint sounds of revelry rise up.*) O most pernicious woman! O villain, villain, smiling damned villain! My tables! (*He drags out his student's commonplace book and begins to write in it feverishly.*) Meet it is I set it down that one may smile and smile and be a villain— so, uncle, there you are! Now to my word. It is, 'Adieu, adieu, remember me!' I have sworn it!
Voices call him from below: My lord, my lord! Lord Hamlet!

Hamlet descends from the platform, and greets his anxious, fearful companions.

MARCELLUS   How is't, my noble lord?

HORATIO   What news, Hamlet?

HAMLET   It is an honest ghost, that let me tell you. For your desire to know what is between us, o'ermaster it as you may. And now good friends, as you are friends, scholars and soldiers, give me one poor request.

HORATIO   What is't, my lord?

HAMLET   Never make known what you have seen tonight.

MARCELLUS AND HORATIO   My lord we will not.

HAMLET   Swear on my sword. (*He holds out his sword. Marcellus and Horatio lay their hands on it and swear. Hamlet now thrusts his sword at them again.*) Here as before, never, so help you mercy, how strange or odd so'er I bear myself, as I perchance hereafter shall think meet to put an antic disposition on, (*He falls into an attitude suggesting madness.*) to note that you know aught of me. Swear.

Much mystified, his companions swear again. Hamlet puts away his sword, and smiles at his friends.

HAMLET   Let us go in together. The time is out of joint, O cursed spite, that ever I was born to set it right.

Hamlet skips ahead of his friends, turns, and adopts his attitude of pretended madness. Then he lays a warning finger to his lips, and shakes his head.

Polonius's apartment in the castle. Polonius is seated at a table. Suddenly his daughter, Ophelia, comes rushing in. It is clear that she is upset.

OPHELIA   O my lord, my lord, I have been so affrighted!

POLONIUS   With what, i' the name of God?

OPHELIA   My lord, as I was sewing in my closet, Lord Hamlet, with his doublet all unbraced, pale as his shirt, his knees knocking each other, and with a look so piteous in purport as if he had been loosed out of hell to speak of horrors, he comes before me!

POLONIUS   Mad for thy love?

OPHELIA   My lord, I do not know, but truly I do fear it.

POLONIUS   (*rising and taking Ophelia firmly by the hand*) Come, go with me. I will go seek the king. This is the very ecstasy of love. (*He looks at her closely.*) Have you given him any hard words of late?

OPHELIA   No, my good lord, but as you did command, I did repel his letters and denied his access to me.

POLONIUS   That hath made him mad. Come, go we to the king.

In the royal apartment, the king and queen are seated, with courtiers in attendance. Polonius and Ophelia appear in the door. Then Polonius, examining the distraught looks of his daughter, decides she is unfit to be brought into the presence of the king. He sends her away and enters on his own.

POLONIUS (*triumphantly*) I have found the very cause of Hamlet's lunacy!

KING O speak of that: that do I long to hear!

QUEEN I doubt it is no other but the main: his father's death and our o'er-hasty marriage.

POLONIUS (*wisely shaking his head*) I will be brief. Your noble son is mad: mad call I it, for to define true madness, what is't but to be nothing else but mad? But let that go.

QUEEN (*impatiently*) More matter with less art.

POLONIUS Madam, I swear I use no art at all. That he's mad 'tis true, 'tis true 'tis pity, and pity 'tis 'tis true—a foolish figure, but farewell it, for I will use no art. Perpend. I have a daughter—have while she is mine—who in her duty and obedience, mark, hath given me this. (*He produces a letter which he reads.*) 'To the celestial, and my soul's idol, the most beautified Ophelia'—That's an ill phrase, a vile phrase, 'beautified' is a vile phrase. But you shall hear: 'O dear Ophelia, I am ill. I have not art to reckon my groans; but that I love thee best, O most best, believe it . . .'

QUEEN   Came this from Hamlet to her?

Polonius nods and gives the queen the letter. She studies it and passes it to the king.

KING   Do you think 'tis this?

QUEEN   It may be; very like.

KING   How may we try it further?

POLONIUS   You know he walks sometimes four hours together here in the lobby? At such a time I'll loose my daughter to him. You and I, behind an arras there, mark the encounter.

KING   We will try it.

Hamlet enters, his dress much disordered. He is reading a book.

QUEEN   But look where sadly the poor wretch comes.

POLONIUS   Away, I do beseech you both. I'll board him presently.

The king and queen, together with the courtiers, depart, leaving Polonius to confront Hamlet.

POLONIUS   How does my good lord Hamlet?

HAMLET   Well, God a-mercy.

POLONIUS   Do you know me, my lord?

HAMLET Excellent well. You are a fishmonger.

POLONIUS Not I, my lord.

HAMLET Then I would you were so honest a man.

POLONIUS Honest, my lord?

HAMLET Ay, sir, to be honest, as this world goes, is to be one man picked out of ten thousand.

POLONIUS That's very true, my lord. (*Aside*) Though this be madness, yet there's method in't.

HAMLET Have you a daughter?

POLONIUS I have, my lord.

HAMLET Let her not walk in the sun. Conception is a blessing, but as your daughter may conceive, friend, look to it.

POLONIUS (*aside*) Still harping on my daughter. Yet he knew me not at first, he said I was a fishmonger. He is far gone. I'll speak to him again. Will you walk out of the air, my lord?

HAMLET Into my grave.

POLONIUS Indeed, that's out of the air. (*Aside*) How pregnant sometimes his replies are! (*To Hamlet*) My lord, I will take my leave of you.

HAMLET You cannot, sir, take from me anything that I will more willingly part withal—except my life, except my life, except my life. (*Polonius bows and withdraws. Hamlet stares contemptuously after him.*) These tedious old fools!

He goes to a window and gazes out. Far below a cart toils up the hill towards the castle. It bears a huge banner on which is written: 'The best actors in the world, either for Comedy, Tragedy, History . . .' In the cart sit the actors themselves, a perfect painted court, not unlike the royal court of Denmark. Hamlet turns away.

HAMLET (*thoughtfully*) I have heard that guilty creatures sitting at a play, have, by the very cunning of the scene, been struck so to the soul that presently they have proclaimed their malefactions! I will have these players play something like the murder of my father before mine uncle. I'll observe his looks. The spirit that I have seen may be a devil—and the devil hath power t'assume a pleasing shape. I'll have grounds more relative than this. The play's the thing wherein I'll catch the conscience of the king!

A lobby in the castle. The king and Polonius together.

They hide in an alcove behind a curtain. Enter Hamlet, reading. He looks up, deeply troubled.

HAMLET   To be, or not to be, that is the question: whether 'tis nobler in the mind to suffer the slings and arrows of outrageous fortune, or to take arms against a sea of troubles, and by opposing, end them. To die, to sleep—no more; and by a sleep to say we end the heartache and the thousand natural shocks that flesh is heir to; 'tis a consummation devoutly to be wished. To die, to sleep—to sleep, perchance to dream—ay, there's the rub, for in that sleep of death what dreams may come, when we have shuffled off this mortal coil, must give us pause . . .

Ophelia approaches.

OPHELIA   Good my lord, how does your honour for this many a day?

HAMLET   I humbly thank you, well, well, well.

OPHELIA   My lord, I have remembrances of yours that I have longed to redeliver. (*She approaches and holds out a bundle of ribbon-tied letters and a necklace.*) Rich gifts wax poor when givers prove unkind. There, my lord.

HAMLET   (*taking the offerings*) I did love you once.

OPHELIA   Indeed, my lord, you made me believe so.

HAMLET   You should not have believed me. I loved you not.

OPHELIA   I was the more deceived.

HAMLET   Get thee to a nunnery. Why, would'st thou be a breeder of sinners? Go thy ways to a nunnery! Where's your father?

OPHELIA   At home, my lord.

HAMLET   Let the doors be shut upon him, that he may play the fool nowhere but in's own house. To a nunnery go, and quickly too! Or if thou wilt needs marry, marry a fool. For wise men know well enough what monsters you make of them.

OPHELIA   Heavenly powers restore him!

HAMLET   I have heard of your paintings well enough. God hath given you one face, and you make yourselves another. You jig and amble, and you lisp, you nickname God's creatures and you make your wantonness your ignorance. Go to, I'll no more on't, it hath made me mad. I say we will have no more marriage. Those that are married already (all but one) shall live, the rest shall keep as they are. To a nunnery, go.

Hamlet flings the keepsakes in the air. Ophelia sinks to the ground. The king and Polonius emerge from concealment.

KING   Love? His affections do not that way tend. There's something in his soul . . . He shall with speed to England. Madness in great ones must not unwatched go.

The Court are all assembled in a great chamber, awaiting the performance of the players. A curtain hides the stage. The king and queen are sitting side by side. Hamlet sits beside Ophelia, and closely observes the king. The king beckons to Hamlet.

KING   Have you heard the argument? Is there no offence in't?

HAMLET   No, no, they do but jest—poison in jest. No offence i'the world!

The king nods. He signs to the musicians. They sound a fanfare. The curtain parts and reveals a painted orchard. The action of the play is carried on in dumbshow, to the accompaniment of music. The Player King and Player Queen come on, and fondly embrace.

The Player King lies down to sleep. The Player Queen draws aside. A murderer enters and cunningly pours poison in the Player King's sleeping ear. The Player King jerks in violent pain; then dies. The Player Queen rushes forward and clasps her dead husband with extravagant grief.

HAMLET   (*to the queen*) Madam, how like you this play?

QUEEN   The lady doth protest too much, methinks.

On the stage, the murderer takes the Player Queen by the arm, and offers her jewels. At first she resists, but then, little by little, she capitulates. The Player Queen and the murderer embrace passionately.

  The king rises from his seat. He is enraged and terrified by the image of his own crime. The court rises in consternation.

HAMLET   What, frighted with false fire?

KING   Give me some light! Away!

He rushes away, followed by the distracted queen and all the court. Hamlet and Horatio are left alone.

HAMLET   O good Horatio, I'll take the ghost's word for a thousand pound. Didst perceive?

HORATIO   Very well, my lord!

Polonius returns, much agitated.

POLONIUS My lord, the queen would speak with you.

HAMLET   I will come to my mother by and by. (*Aside*) I will speak daggers to her but use none.

In the queen's bedchamber. Polonius attempts to give counsel to the queen.

POLONIUS Look you lay home to him, tell him his pranks have been too broad to bear with. Pray you be round!

QUEEN   Fear me not. Withdraw, I hear him coming!

Hastily, Polonius conceals himself behind a curtain. Hamlet enters, wild of aspect.

HAMLET   How now, mother, what's the matter?

QUEEN   Hamlet, thou hast thy father much offended.

HAMLET   Mother, you have my father much offended.

QUEEN   Come, come, you answer with an idle tongue.

HAMLET   Go, go, you question with a wicked tongue.

He stares at her menacingly. She retreats. He seizes her and forces her to sit on the bed.

HAMLET   Come, come, you shall not budge—

QUEEN   What wilt thou do? Thou wilt not murder me? Help, ho!

POLONIUS   *(behind the curtain)* What ho! Help!

HAMLET   *(rushing to the curtain)* How now? A rat! Dead for a ducat, dead! *(He thrusts his sword through the curtain. There is a cry, and the sound of a body falling. Hamlet draws out his bloody sword. He looks to the queen.)* Is it the King? *(He draws aside the curtain, and sees Polonius, dead.)*

QUEEN O what a rash and bloody deed is this!

HAMLET *(to the dead Polonius)* Thou wretched, rash, intruding fool, farewell; I took thee for thy better. Thou find'st to be too busy is some danger. *(To the queen)* Leave wringing your hands. Peace, sit you down, and let me wring your heart. *(They sit, side by side, on the bed. Hamlet holds up a locket he wears round his neck and shows it to his mother.)* Look here upon this picture, *(He drags a locket from his mother's neck and compares it with the other.)* and on this, the counterfeit presentment of two brothers. Have you eyes? Could you on this fair mountain feed and batten on this moor? Ha, have you eyes? You cannot call it love, for at your age the heyday in the blood is tame, it's humble and waits upon the judgement, and what judgement would step from this to this?

QUEEN   O speak to me no more. These words like daggers enter in my ears!

HAMLET   A murderer and a villain—

QUEEN   No more!

HAMLET   A king of shreds and patches—

Suddenly, the ghost appears. Hamlet stares at it, wild-eyed.

QUEEN   Alas, he's mad!

HAMLET   (*to ghost*) Do you not come your tardy son to chide?

GHOST   Do not forget. This visitation is to whet thy almost blunted purpose. But look, amazement on thy mother sits. Speak to her, Hamlet.

HAMLET   How is't with you, lady?

QUEEN   Alas, how is't with you? Whereon do you look?

HAMLET   On him, on him! Look you how pale he glares! Do you see nothing there?

QUEEN   Nothing at all—

HAMLET   Nor did you nothing hear?

QUEEN   No, nothing but ourselves!

The ghost begins to depart . . .

HAMLET   Why, look you there, look how it steals away, my father in his habit as he lived! Look where he goes!

QUEEN   This is the very coinage of your brain . . .

Hamlet shakes his head. He rises and goes to the dead Polonius.

HAMLET   This man shall send me packing. I'll lug the guts into the neighbour room. This counsellor is now most still, most secret, and most grave, who was in life a foolish prating knave. (*He seizes hold of the dead man's feet and begins to drag him to the door.*) Come, sir, draw toward an end with you. Good night, mother.

Hamlet departs with the body. The king enters, followed by his attendants.

KING   How does Hamlet?

QUEEN   Mad as the sea and wind. In his lawless fit, behind the arras hearing something stir, whips out his rapier, cries 'A rat, a rat!' and kills the unseen good old man!

KING   O heavy deed! Where is he gone?

QUEEN   To draw apart the body—

KING   (*to attendants*) Go seek him out!

The body of Polonius has not been found; but Hamlet has been seized and brought before the king.

KING   Now, Hamlet, where's Polonius?

HAMLET   At supper.

KING   At supper? Where?

HAMLET   Not where he eats, but where he's eaten; a certain convocation of politic worms are e'en at him.

KING   Where is Polonius?

HAMLET   In heaven, send thither to see; if your messenger find him not there, seek him i' the other place yourself. But if indeed you find him not within this month, you shall nose him as you go up the stairs into the lobby.

KING   (*to attendants*) Go seek him there. (*To Hamlet*) Hamlet, this deed must send thee hence. Therefore prepare thyself for England. (*Hamlet shrugs his shoulders and departs. The king looks after him savagely.*) England, if my love thou holds at aught, thou mayst not coldly set our sovereign process, which imports at full, by letters congruing to that effect, the present death of Hamlet! Do it, England, for like the hectic in my blood he rages, and thou must cure me!

In the royal apartment, the king and queen look to one another in dismay as a strange, distracted wailing is heard. Ophelia enters, all in ragged white, crying and laughing and singing. Wild flowers are in her hair, and she carries a posy. The death of her father and the loss of Hamlet have driven her mad.

OPHELIA   (*singing*)   He is dead and gone, lady,
He is dead and gone . . .   (*She drifts away.*)

KING   O Gertrude, Gertrude, when sorrows come, they come not single spies, but in battalions . . .

There is a violent commotion outside. A soldier enters.

SOLDIER   Save yourself, my lord! Young Laertes in riotous head o'erbears your officers! The rabble call him lord!

Laertes with armed followers, bursts in.

LAERTES   (*to followers*) Sirs, stand you all without! O thou vile king, give me my father!

QUEEN   Calmly, good Laertes. (*She tries to restrain him.*)

KING   Let him go, Gertrude, do not fear our person. There's such divinity doth hedge a king that treason can but peep at what it would. Tell me, Laertes, why thou art thus incensed?

LAERTES Where is my father?

KING Dead.

QUEEN But not by him!

KING I am guiltless of thy father's death, and am—

He breaks off as a sound of strange singing is heard.

LAERTES What noise is that?

Ophelia returns, in her distracted state. Laertes stares at her in horror.

OPHELIA They bore him bare-faced on the bier
And on his grave rained many a tear—

She stops, and, plucking flowers from her posy, presents them to Laertes.

OPHELIA There's rosemary, that's for remembrance. (*To the queen*) There's fennel for you, and columbines. (*To the king*) There's rue for you. And here's some for me. We may call it herb o' grace on Sundays. You must wear your rue with a difference. I would give you some violets, but they withered all when my father died. They say he made a good end.

All watch her, filled with pity. Laertes weeps for his sister.

OPHELIA   (*singing*)

> And will he not come again,
> And will he not come again?
> No, no, he's dead,
> Go to thy deathbed,
> He never will come again.

She drifts out of the apartment, out of the castle and into the woods beyond, until she comes to a stream, and there, still singing, clambers onto the branch of a willow, which breaks and casts her into the brook. 'Her clothes spread wide, and mermaid-like awhile they bore her up. But long it could not be till that her garments, heavy with their drink, pulled the poor wretch from her melodious lay to muddy death.'

The ship taking Hamlet to England has been attacked by pirates; and Hamlet, discovering the plot against his life, has boarded the pirate vessel and, in exchange for promises of reward, has been landed safely once more on Danish soil. He and Horatio are together, near to a churchyard. As they approach, they see a gravedigger at work, and singing.

GRAVEDIGGER

> In youth when I did love, did love,
> Methought it was very sweet . . .

HAMLET   Hath this fellow no feeling for his business? He sings in grave-making. (*He addresses the grave-digger*) What man dost thou dig for?

GRAVEDIGGER	For no man, sir.
HAMLET	For what woman then?
GRAVEDIGGER	For none neither.
HAMLET	Who is to be buried in it?
GRAVEDIGGER	One that was a woman, sir; but rest her soul, she's dead. (*He picks up a skull from the earth*.) Here's a skull now hath lien you i' the earth three-and-twenty years.
HAMLET	Whose was it?
GRAVEDIGGER	A whoreson mad fellow's it was! This same skull, sir, was Yorick's skull, the King's jester.

Hamlet takes the skull and gazes at it wonderingly.

HAMLET	This?
GRAVEDIGGER	E'en that.
HAMLET	Alas, poor Yorick, I knew him, Horatio, a fellow of infinite jest. (*To the skull*) No one now to mock your own grinning? Now get you to my lady's chamber, and tell her, let her paint an inch thick, to this favour she must come. Let her laugh at that. But soft, here comes the King, the Queen, the courtiers!

A funeral procession approaches. The king, queen, Laertes, and all the court follow a coffin. A priest is in attendance. Hamlet and Horatio withdraw behind a monument, to watch. The procession reaches the grave, and the coffin is lowered in. The priest turns away.

LAERTES   Must there be no more done? (*The priest shakes his head.*) I tell thee, churlish priest, a ministering angel shall my sister be when thou liest howling!

HAMLET   What, the fair Ophelia!

QUEEN   (*scattering flowers on the coffin*) Sweets to the sweet. Farewell.

LAERTES   Hold off the earth awhile, till I have caught her once more in mine arms!

He leaps down into the grave. Hamlet rushes upon the scene.

HAMLET   What is he whose grief bears such an emphasis?

LAERTES   (*looking up*) The devil take thy soul!

Hamlet leaps down into the grave and grapples with Laertes.

KING   Pluck them asunder!

QUEEN   Hamlet, Hamlet!

HAMLET   I loved Ophelia! Forty thousand brothers could not with all
          their quantity of love make up my sum!

KING   O he is mad, Laertes!

QUEEN   For love of God, forbear him!

*Courtiers drag the warring youths apart. They glare at each
other. Then Hamlet shrugs his shoulders.*

HAMLET   Hear you, sir, what is the reason you use me thus? I loved you
          ever—but it is no matter. Let Hercules himself do what he may,
          the cat will mew, and dog will have his day.

An apartment in the castle. The king and Laertes are together.

KING   Hamlet comes back; what would you undertake in deed to
          show yourself your father's son?

LAERTES   To cut his throat i' the church.

KING   (*nodding*) Will you be ruled by me?

LAERTES   Ay, my lord.

KING   You have been talked of since your travel much, and that in Hamlet's hearing, for a quality wherein they say you shine.

LAERTES   What part is that?

KING   For art and exercise in your defence, and for your rapier most especial. This report did Hamlet so envenom with his envy that he could do nothing but wish and beg your sudden coming o'er to play with you.

LAERTES   What out of this, my lord?

KING   Bring you in fine together, and wager on your heads. He being remiss, and free from all contriving, will not peruse the foils, so that with ease, or with a little shuffling, you may choose a sword unbated, and in a pass of practice requite him for your father!

LAERTES   (*eagerly*) I will do't, and for that purpose I'll anoint my sword. I bought an unction from a mountebank, so mortal that but to dip a knife in it . . . (*He makes an expressive gesture, indicating sudden death.*)

KING   Let's think further of this. When in your motion you are hot and dry, as make your bouts more violent to that end, and that he calls for drink, I'll have prepared him a chalice for the nonce, whereon but sipping, if he by chance escape your venomed stuck, our purpose may hold there.

They gaze into one another's eyes, deeply.

The great hall of the castle. Hamlet and Horatio are together. The fencing match with Laertes has been agreed to. A courtier enters.

COURTIER My lord, his majesty sends to know if your pleasure hold to play with Laertes.

HAMLET I am constant to my purpose. (*The courtier bows and departs.*)

HORATIO You will lose, my lord.

HAMLET I do not think so. But thou would'st not think how ill all's here about my heart—but no matter.

HORATIO If your mind dislike anything, obey it. I will forestall their repair hither and say you are not fit.

HAMLET We defy augury. There is special providence in the fall of a sparrow. The readiness is all. Let be.

Trumpets sound, heralding the approach of the king and queen, and all the court, to witness the fencing-match. They seat themselves. Foils are brought forward. They are offered first to Laertes. He chooses one, and flourishes it.

LAERTES This is too heavy. Let me see another.

He takes another, which suits him better. He exchanges a secret nod with the king while Hamlet chooses a sword for himself.

HAMLET   This likes me well.

A servant brings a goblet of wine and sets it beside the king.

KING   Come, begin. And you, the judges, bear a wary eye.

The adversaries' swords are put together.

HAMLET   Come on, sir!

They fence. Hamlet scores a hit.

JUDGE   A hit, a very palpable hit!

The duellists part. The king frowns. He drops something in the goblet.

KING   Hamlet, this pearl is thine! Give him the cup!

HAMLET   I'll play this bout first. Set it by awhile. Come. (*They fence again. Again Hamlet scores a hit.*) Another hit, what say you?

LAERTES   I do confess't.

KING   (*to queen*) Our son shall win.

QUEEN   Here, Hamlet, take my napkin, rub thy brows. (*She takes up the goblet.*) The Queen carouses to thy fortune, Hamlet!

KING   Gertrude, do not drink!

QUEEN	I will, my lord, I pray you pardon me. (*She drinks.*)
KING	(*aside*) It is the poisoned cup! It is too late.
QUEEN	(*to Hamlet*) Come, let me wipe your face.

Hamlet goes to his mother, Laertes lunges at him and wounds his arm. Hamlet turns, incensed. They begin to fence again, but with a deadly fury. Suddenly Laertes is disarmed. Hamlet takes up the fallen sword, stares at its unbated tip. He throws his own sword to Laertes, and with the poisoned weapon begins to fight again. Laertes is wounded.

SERVANT	Look to the Queen!

The fighting stops. The queen has fallen back. She is dying.

KING	She swoons to see them bleed!
QUEEN	No, no, the drink, the drink! O my dear Hamlet! The drink, the drink! I am poisoned! (*She dies.*)
HAMLET	O villainy! Let the door be locked! Treachery, seek it out!

He rushes at the king. The court seeks to fly from the scene. Laertes has fallen. His wound is bleeding.

LAERTES   It is here, Hamlet. Hamlet, thou art slain, no medicine in the world can do thee good, in thee there is not half an hour of life. The treacherous instrument is in thine hand, unbated and envenomed. The foul practice hath turned itself on me. The King—the King's to blame!

Hamlet seizes the king and stabs him with the poisoned blade.

HAMLET   Venom, do thy work! (*He takes hold of the poisoned goblet and forces its contents down the king's throat.*) Here, thou incestuous, murderous, damned Dane, drink off this potion! Follow my mother! (*The king dies.*)

LAERTES   Exchange forgiveness with me, noble Hamlet.

Hamlet takes his offered hand. Then Laertes, doomed like all who had touched the corruption of the state, dies.

HAMLET   Heaven make thee free of it. I follow thee. (*He staggers.
Horatio comes to support him.*) I am dead, Horatio. (*He tries
to embrace the dead queen.*) Wretched Queen, adieu. (*He
almost falls, and Horatio eases him into the chair from which
the king has fallen.*) This fell sergeant, Death, is strict in his
arrest. If thou didst ever hold me in thy heart, absent thee from
felicity awhile, and in this harsh world draw thy breath in pain
to tell my story . . . (*He tries to smile.*) The rest is silence . . .
(*He dies.*)

HORATIO   Now cracks a noble heart. Good night, sweet prince, and
flights of angels sing thee to thy rest.

The curtain falls . . .